T0159133

Poetic Thoughts in the Keys of Happiness

NURTURING INSPIRATIONS FOR EVERY WOMAN

B A M

Table of Contents

Part III. Questioning it All! Does True Love Really Exist?

Part IV. If You Dwell on Yesterday, Tomorrow may Never Come or be Visualized

Part V. Take Me To The Next Phase, Keeping It REAL!!!

Part VI. Poetic Thoughts of Dedications and Bereavements to family and friends

Acknowledgement

The dedication of this book is in the loving memory of my loving parents H.T. and Marjorie Murray, my sister Emma, whom we tragically lost to bone cancer in 2007, and my twelve (11) siblings: Annie Ruth, Rosie, Eddie, Patty, Linda, Ray Charles, Milton, Cathy, Rita, Robert and Hayden.

To my daughter Tisa, (Husband) Carneil Brooks and my lovely granddaughter Sophia Olivia Brooks "I love you guys so much". Always love each other and Sophia.

There is a special acknowledgment to my cousin Bishop Gaines, Shirley Gaines, and all my friends that were there for me during the worst part of my life, my divorce.

To my travelling colleague and best friend Linda J. Reeves, you are truly the epitome of a great friend. May God continue to bless you all?

My Heroes

(special tribute to my five wonderful brothers)

My Heroes are my 5 brothers
They are superbly like no other.
Eddie. Ray, Milton, Robert , and June.
Are Brothers that are family oriented and in tune.
They are serious, wonderful, forgiving, and handy.
Serving our Country with pride and doing numerous tours of duty
You are **Men** of character that's absolutely dandy.

SOPHIA

Sophia, You are like an angel that flew down to Earth.
You brought our family so much joy at the time of your birth
One look in your bright eyes, none of us were ever the same.
Because you became a living doll each time we called your name.
There is a part in my heart and a bond that won't ever sever,
Sophia, you are our baby, our angel, and I'm sure along with your mom, dad, grandpa, and grandma's, uncles and aunts, nieces, and nephews as well as your favorite cousin kenzie and others we will all love and support you forever!

Sophia, you are more perfect than I could have hoped, your personality is more beautiful than we ever dreamed.
Each day you are more precious that anyone could have imagined,
That's why I love you more than I could have ever
Known . . . .

(Especially for you, from Glam-ma)

(To my One and Only Child , I Love You more than Life, and wish you the very best in all your endeavors . . . . always Mom)

For my Daughter I would

TEE, for you I would climb
Mt. Everest highest peak
Swim the depth of the Pacific ocean
To capture the love of a daughter so meek.

Baby, for you I would crown you queen
And place upon your head the biggest crown
To fulfill a smile that's a mile wide
Just to know that you will always be by my side.

You are a daughter, O' so beautiful
Giving birth to you was a radical experience.
The moment the nurse place you in my arms
Your eyes lit up like a luminous light,
We could tell then that you would be ever so bright.
I pray that you never take your love away
For I reassure I love you every day
For you I would . . .
If I could
Make you the one
Who makes me whole
Because your birth captured my heart
. . . . and touched my soul

Family Portrait

Celebrating Family at Reunion

Enjoying Family Gathering and Spreading Good Cheer

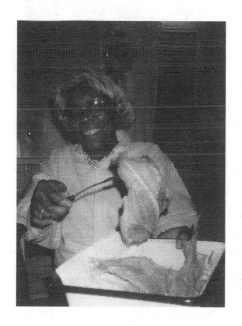

$\mathcal{P}$reface

This book is written in poetic form about relationships of unrequited love, love that went awry, and trying to make connections to a future partner. It also contain some personal experiences with several acquaintances, based on what I want in a partner, how to win his heart and an expansive view of my life and my passions. Names have been altered to protect the innocent and the guilty.

The middle portion of the book questions if there is really true love, can it be found, and vows of love that will make your heart melt. My journey of completeness encapsulates getting over that person in the past by moving on and not living in the past, because if you live in Yesterday, your Tomorrow may never be visualized or realized.

"Take Me To The Next Phase Baby" is a synopsis of meeting someone and keeping it real. The ond of the book arbitrarily deals with dedications and the death of two brothers that occurred 2 days apart and was written for each of their sisters who happens to be my very best friends, Violia and Dianne. May the memories of Ernie and Arthur supersede the wonderful times and great experiences you shared with your families.

Love Always,
Barbara

My Philosophy of Education

I would be remised not to mention my philosophy of education since I spent (37) years in the classroom. I would like to briefly describe my personal feelings and beliefs as a teacher including my perception of what makes an outstanding teacher.

Being a classroom teacher is one of the most rewarding jobs on the planet, because every profession such as doctors, lawyers, engineers, pilots, nurses and even the highest office in the land, our Presidents owe homage to educators for cultivating their learning professions.

My concepts of what makes an outstanding teacher is one that is imaginative, effective, supportive, and dedicated. An outstanding teacher implores critical thinking skills, use teaching strategies with the use of technology orientation, and have many schemas for solving certain kinds of problems.

My philosophy of education implores that "all children can learn if they are provided an enriched atmosphere conducive to learning. I believe that the lst steps to learning consist of attitude and perception. In other words a child must possess a positive attitude to learn before he/she can perceive learning, integrate, or acquire new knowledge. I believe that the second step to learning is prior knowledge, being able to analyze in depth what has already been previously learned. I direct my thinking to the views of Gardner's (MI) Multiple Intelligence theories and Piaget's theories of cognitive development. After all, on this vast planet there are no two students alike, therefore; people learn using a variety of many different dimensions and strategies. In my classroom, I encouraged all my students to help each other (Buddy Learning) and not make fun when someone is having difficulties in a certain area.

I found teaching to be one o f the most rewarding tasks I've ever done. If just one student soars to utopia height, it was a grand feeling. When I taught math and introduced a new math concept all I want to hear was one student express "oh, I got It!" or see the expression on their face with a smile saying "I can do it now!" That expression was like winning a 6 million dollar lottery.

Excerpts of my Impassable journey

My impassable journey has been a treacherous up hill battle, with many obstacles that have been close calls and several near death episodes. (This is also the title of my second book).

My journey began in the red clay hills of Georgia on a military Reservation about 15 miles south of Ft. Benning, Georgia. Our home was extremely close to the military reservation, to the point that we could look out of our dining room window and see the military Maneuvers. We were unable to play in the backyard due to the shooting and range practices. The metal casings from the rifles would fly into our back yard and could be found in the wood piles near the reservation. We would watch the soldiers do their maneuvers and drills each day and leave.

During the summer months my brothers would collect the metal shell casings from the M-16 rifles and other weapons used. We would collect bags of shell casings and sell them at the scrap metal yards.

I come from a very large family, twelve siblings, we would use the money collected for the metal shell casings to purchase school lunch. My mother would make our daily lunches so when we had money we would buy lunch and give the home made lunches to our friends. (But mom didn't know this)

As a child I was constantly fighting for my life. I had severe Asthma attacks, many times unable to catch my breath. I could not lie flat in the bed and sleep like a normal kid. I had to be propped upright on many pillows to be able to breathe. I remember being hospitalized fifteen (15) times in one year with chronic asthma attacks and would miss numerous days from school.

During each attacks my mother often thought it was going to be my last breath in that my grandfather had asthma very bad also and eventually died of an asthma attack.

My father was a contractor on the military base, a missionary Minister and my mother was a great gospel singer, with a beautiful voice. They both worked at Fort

Benning and were very anointed and praying parents. They prayed often for God to heal me from the evil of these vicious asthma attacks. Their prayers were truly answered by the time I was seventeen and a half years old, the attacks curtailed immensely and eventually faded away.

The asthma attacks were said to have stunted my growth, which is perhaps why I'm five feet zero inches tall? Eventually, by the time I turned twenty (20) the attacks just abruptly stopped. I also had a heart murmur, severe menstrual cramps called endometritis. The cramps would cause me to pass out in the streets or in the playground. I had to be accompanied by a sibling or cousin at all times due to the severity of the cramps.

In the early sixties my father developed lung cancer, which was diagnosed as a result of asbestos and perhaps Agent Orange from being a contractor on the military base. The doctors summoned the whole family and told my mother that my father had (2) months to live. But the devil turned into a big liar, my dad lived thirteen (I3) years after this diagnosis. The cancer went into remission, but years later showed up in his stomach and entire body.

What happened next was unspeakable; I got that fateful call that my father had a relapse and the cancer was metastasizing throughout his stomach, and entire body. I waited a week before going home thinking he would get better like he did before. Finally, I got a call from my mother stating I needed to get home if I expected to see him alive. So I boarded a plane home the next day. Upon landing my brother was waiting at the airport for me with news I wasn't prepared to hear. He stated my father had gone from I50 pounds in weight to a mere 65 pounds. I was totally speechless. We drove to the hospital in complete silence. As we were rushing into the hospital entrance, we met my aunt coming down the hall. Daddy had taken his last breath and expired before I could get to his room. The fact that everyone told me he tried to "hold on" for me was comforting, but by now I was livid and completely devastated. I wanted to crawl in the hospital bed and have the undertaker place us both in the same body bag.

My father and I was thicker than two thieves, he allowed me to do everything with him. Every one viewed me as my daddy's favorite. We went to church every Sunday and sometimes I would sit up front with him when he led devotion.

Daddy was also an A-I Mechanic. When he worked on cars I was a grease monkey too. I would be there under the car handing him tools or whatever gadget he needed. We would also sneak off in the car once we repaired it to get ice cream or visit his best friend or cousins. At the age of 5 years old I was sitting in his lap driving and drag racing. One day when I was seven, I was behind the wheel driving when I suddenly crashed our 1957 Ford in to his cousin's Model T Ford. It was my first official car accident. The police was not called because my dad and I assessed the damages and agreed to repair both cars.

After the death of my father, my mom and aunts tried to comfort me but nothing anyone said made a difference. I was a "Daddy's Girl," all I could think of was the week I delayed returning home, thinking he would get better. I beat myself up very badly knowing that I could have avoided this scenario if I had boarded the plane a week earlier. No one in the universe could imagine my devastation of pure guilt.

What was I going to do? How was my mother going to survive raising 10 siblings that were still living at home? Should I leave my job and not return to the Federal Center in Colorado?

I was boldly questioning God, how could he take my father away at thirty nine (39) years old and not take some of the drunken bums on the street with worthless lives? My father had demonstrated his faith in God and chose to do his will. Yet, I felt like God didn't treat him right. I felt that God had been mean and evil against me. It was my belief that God was suppose to allow good things to happen to the people that worshipped him like my father. Was I losing my sense of religion? Did God really have direct influence on healing and how did he select the people he delivered? My father praised God for all eternity and enjoyed praising him even in the in the midst of all his pain.

At this moment I no longer thought that praising God was a magical incantation because he could not stop the cancer from victimizing my father's body. I felt that God should have done more. My father was the most gentle and kindest man on the planet. He always had a big smile on his face, and never had anything unkind to say about anyone. In my opinion, and many other people that knew my dad, he was the closest man ever to a Saint or a Pope. By nightfall the day before the funeral, I had worked myself into a real Frenzy, I was completely freaking out and my mom decided I needed to go to the hospital ER Department. The doctor in the ER room took one strong look at me and prescribed a heavy dose of valium for me. No matter how hard I tried I could not get my life together. I decided to leave my job in Denver and stick around to help my mom out with my siblings. A year later I was still taking narcotics. Was I a dumb ole drug addict like the freaks on the street corner that I despised? News started surfacing about Betty Ford's addiction to prescription drug, Elizabeth Taylor and several other celebrities. I became paranoid. I hated drugs, alcohol and smoking, and made a vow to my dad that I would never do any drugs, I've kept that promise to him and myself. So what was happening to me? Deep within my psyche I knew I detested drugs and I could not die as a result of prescription drugs. I knew then and there I had to take myself to another phase and get my life together, I did and until this day I'm still afraid of prescription drugs, especially narcotics. I won't allow myself to take them longer that four to five days no matter what illness is defined.

In my early teens, my mother packed up the family and moved to Cleveland, Ohio to be near my father's family.

Another event of my impassable journey was my battle with Diabetes in 1996. This was a very stressful time in that I was in the beginning stage of my divorce. I was at work when suddenly people started to tell me that I looked strange or my eyes were too glassy. After I ate lunch I really felt like I was transforming into someone else. So I decided to ask my boss if I could leave work and go to the hospital to get myself checked. Luckily I made it through the gate and as I attempted to park, my car jumped the curb and my driver side door flew open. I found myself slumped over the steering wheel and heard several people in the parking lot screaming for help. I remember a burly security guard picking me up and carrying me into the ER Room. When I finally came around I was surrounded by oxygen in my nostrils, tubes and IV's running through my veins. I was told my blood sugar level was up to 860, the doctors were amazed I wasn't in a diabetic comma. God's glory and blessings had saved me from the agony of death. I spent thirteen days in Mercer Hospital with the doctors and nurses trying to regulate my blood sugar, but to no avail. With God, nothing is accidental, in his own power he had held my breadth for life and my destiny. When I was released from the hospital I was taking five different types of insulin a day for survival; 10 units of humalog before and after each meal, 50 units of a 24 hour insulin called Lantus in the morning, 10 units of Byetta twice a day, 20 units of symlin a day, and 20 units of Levemir at bedtime. I was at my wits taking insulin and felt like I had no control over my life. So I became very health conscious and decided to spend several weeks at Better Living Life Style Center learning how to properly detoxify my body and how to eat nutritious vegan meals. This resulted in weight loss and the road to recovery. Now I only take two insulins a day and some days I can go without taking any. I am trying my best to be insulin free by 2014. In 2002, I was diagnosed with pre-cancerous lesions in my cervical area. All glory to God my oncologist was able to catch it in time, even though there are times when I feel it might return without warning.

In 2004, I developed severe carpal tunnel syndrome in my left hand and had to undergo major surgery. The surgery left me completely incapacitated and sent me into a deep depression. They had to cut deep into my tendons to repair the damage. This surgery was during the deep cold winter in New Jersey in January.

Many nights I would sit on my sofa with blankets and comforters wrapped around my body to keep from freezing to death, in that I had difficulties dressing myself. One night my feet were so cold I could not pull my socks upon my feet. I must have cried for hours. I had no immediately relatives living in New Jersey in that my family and siblings still resides in Cleveland, Ohio.

I had meet a nice Haitian male on my job that did not live too far away. So I called him and he became a great helper during my time of need. Twice a week he would stop by to check on me, bring food and even cleaned my home. During this worst moment of my life I realized and discovered that I had more true male friends than females.

In 2008, I had two accidents within nine months apart. January 16, 2008, I fell in the parking lot on black ice, I crashed on both knees. I received a menisar tear in both knees plus a damaged patella bone in my right knee, and injured my right hand causing the flare-up of the worst carpal tunnel my doctor has ever seen. I also tore my right rotator cuff and had to have major surgery.

On November 10, 2008, my life almost came to an abrupt end. I was involved in a near fatal car crash, We were driving back home from Cleveland, Ohio. My sister-in-law was driving when she spotted a large dear in the road. She swerved to avoid the deer and our car careened into the concrete medium strip at approximately 65 miles per hours and flipped over on the highway. Then we were hit by three other cars that felt like we were flipping over and over. I was trapped in the roof of the car still in my sling from the rotator cuff surgery. My sister-in-law was trapped on the floor under the steering column. She had taken off her seatbelt to help me down from the roof because I was being squeezed to death by the seatbelt. Just as she unfasten her belt we were hit by a SUV, the impact penned her completely under the steering wheel. I was being choked to death by the seatbelt and suddenly the delayed airbag exploded and the metal trim went completely through my left cheek and came out through my chin. By now the car was on fire, a truck driver was able to cut my seat belt and drag me out thru the window. Pieces of Glass were enlodged in my head, face and various parts of my body. My face looked like it had been through a meat grinder, blood was everywhere. The fire department arrived just in time to spray white foam into the gas tank and all over the car to avoid an explosion.

While at the hospital, we learned later on, from the police Officers that this was the worst accident on the Pa Turnpike in I8 years without a fatality. We both were taken to Lancaster General Trauma Center.

After 31 years of teaching I continued to go to work in excruciating pain every day. During the day I taught 2nd grade and committed myself to helping them succeed despite the challenges they faced. At the end of my school day I would travel into some of the roughest neighborhood to tutor students who have been expelled, suspended, or who were just too ill to attend school. For three years after my accidents, I committed myself to my job and tirelessly. I gave all I had each and every day. I constantly endured pain and humiliation going to work wearing Flip flops in the winter time because the pain in my foot was so severe I could not wear closed shoes. After visiting a podiatrist, I learned that I had been walking around with a hole in my tabular bone in my left ankle. I was told that if I didn't get it taken care of I would be jacked up in a brace the rest of my life. My principal was very impossible to work for. It was inconceivable what I was going through by now just trying to do my job. So I had a talk with God and some family members. My family convinced me to give up the job and go into retirement. I had over thirty two years invested under contract and three years as a substitute. I decided to scheduled surgery for my foot and went into retirement. I am currently enjoying spending time with my grandbaby and enjoying my life at 62 in Retirement.

Hayden T. Murray—A special Thanks daddy for providing me with a threshold of wonderful adventures. You motivated me to be all that I could be and instilled in me to "Do unto others as I shall have them do unto me". I loved you more than life and I know that you are enjoying heaven because you were the best Dad ever and better than any human Saint or Pope that walked the Earth.

Marjorie H. Murray—Your Praise and Worship Voice were so Angelic. Your spiritual values were massive and made a big difference in our upbringing. You taught us to always stand for something to avoid falling for anything—I understand this motto now more than I did growing up and attributes your persistence, vigor and supportive tenderness to everything that I've become today—Watching you raise my 10 sibling alone after the death of my father is truly a testament that you were "One" of God's chosen ones and a **strong black woman**.

PART I

Poetic Thoughts about Relationships and all About Me

Greetings, A Little about me

Greetings, and thank you for taking a look at my life. I am a fun, upbeat, passionate woman who loves life and all its pursuits. I am always with positive energy and spirit. I try to see the good in every situation, but yet I remain a realist. I am a lover of life. I am open minded, non-judgmental and honest.

I believe in open and honest communication between partners. Without that you have nothing or nothing that you would want to hold on too. I am adventurous as well as playful with a great sense of humor. Sometimes I'm told my humor is razor sharp, but unlike a knife it doesn't cut.

I enjoy honeymooning on cruises, traveling to interesting places like the Grand Canyon, Caverns, and mountains enjoying Mother Nature. I am very outdoorsy, but I am told I clean up very well in that I'm called a "Fashionista"

I like picnics, walking in parks, hiking, biking and backyard barbecues. Amusement parks bring out the kid in me, I love the wildest rides. I like museums, jazz festivals or live concerts, dining out, or dining in. I love live Broadway type plays as well. Of course, nothing beats being home talking and enjoying each others company,

So be the REAL woman not seeking boys but a real man.

Do not fall for the game player or someone representing the image of a man. Enjoy the experience from my book, but to reap excellent results, STAY FOCUSED!!!!!!!!!

All about me

. . . I am a professional Afro-eccentric sister. I am very gentle and a peace loving woman. I am seeking a serious relationship and hopefully the person to spend the rest of our lives together. I enjoy traveling to exotic Islands and going out to interesting places together. I strongly believe that the happiest thing in life is to be happily and faithfully in love. I don't cheat and won't tolerate cheating. I believe God has a lifetime partner for each of us and I believe the Lord will find the man of my dreams.

I originally grew up near Fort Benning, Georgia, 30 minutes from Columbus, Georgia and One and one half hours from Atlanta, later my family moved to Cleveland, Ohio. At sixteen I relocated to McKinney, Texas to attend trade school. I later spent time in Albuquerque, New Mexico, Denver, Colorado and finally settled in Hamilton, New Jersey which borders the Tri States Delaware, Philadelphia, and New York. I have been living in New Jersey most of my adult life and Professional Life.

I am a very open and a straight forward person. I have a strong sense of family and community. I believe in developing a good friendship with a man first. After a friendship has been established, and if the chemistry is right, that friendship can serve as a foundation for developing a more meaningful relationship.

I feel that relationships don't always have to be an all or none proposition. I strongly believe that even if the romance does not deepen or blossom into something very special, at the very least you still have been enriched by the friendship of that individual.

I believe it is healthier to appreciate what's good and positive about a relationship, than to obsess about what is not perfect about it. Having said that, I don't mean that negatively.

My father always said that the strength of a man is God fearing! "Because the strength of a man isn't how many women he has loved, its in how true he can be to the one woman he's trying to love . . . . and if he can't be true to the one he is trying to love there can never be the blossoming of a meaningful relationship . . . ."

I am independent, ambitious, witty, adventurous and self sufficient, but not to the point that I won't accept your invitation for conversation, coffee, or dinner. I have a great sense of humor and would like the same from my partner. I have healed from my past relationship and I'm ready to move forward toward a healthy, affectionate, and passionate romance. I prefer a man that is self sufficient and independent, not selfish, God fearing, and has his own sense of self and identity, feels good about himself and knows how to make his woman feel the same. I am willing to create, build a life that's acceptable for the quest of life we both hope to share. If you are

And know what you stand for . . . . then seek your love one.

I am

I am a strong black woman
I am a good woman.
I know good women are not finished.
I am a God-fearing woman looking for a God-fearing man.
God has a lifetime partner for each of his children.
I am a believer on the Lord and that he will always find a way.

Relationships

Relationships are a constant work in progress
Without great communication it can lead to serious duress
Life is a gift—so live it to the its fullest
Nothing is a given in this life
So inspire, create a positive attitude without strife
Because the difference between what you want and
what you have
Is truly the effort and sacrifice you endeavor to achieve it.
Relationships can be frightening
But delightful!
So don't let a frugal one get in the way of living your life to its fullest.
With the right attitude and your best efforts it can be the greatest.
Never let an uninspiring relationship slow you down
Sometimes laughter is the best medicine and can put you
On the path of happiness without a frown
A relationship is meeting someone who enjoys spending quality time
With me as much as I would like with them
So set aside your fear and guilt from a failed relationship
Since it really would not matter to me what we do, as long as
we are doing things together

I Want A Friend First

*****<u>*EJ, Just wanted to let you know what I'm about, I'm still anticipating meeting you on your visit that is if you are still interested in meeting me after reading this introduction.*</u>

I want a friend first, that loves his mother, father or grandmother/grandfather and knows how to treat a woman with respect. I need someone who is spiritual filled (loves the Lord) a good listener, stable both emotional and financial. Someone who knows that a woman is to be loved and cherished in every aspect. One who knows that a woman will not change to be someone she is not. I'm a woman that is honest and true to her words with no hidden secrets. (Not that I'm aware of) I know how to take care of my responsibilities and how to let a man be himself and not judge him because he is confident, strong, spoiled and knows how to work for a living. I'm not hung up on what type of job you do, nor what's in your wallet, its just important that you have a wallet and works. I need a good communicator who knows the different between personality and character. One who knows the qualities to look for in a friendship before it becomes a relationship.

I'd just like to seriously add . . . .

During the last four years of my divorce and being totally alone, I have learned how to adapt and overcome many things that I perhaps took for granted in the past and I know that love is not enough to make a relationship work; it needs the 3C's compatibility, commitment, communication and most importantly God in your life. My business and careers are important to me and to know that I love myself first before I can love someone else. I enjoy traveling and healing through natural health. I don't do drugs of any kind nor alcohol and would like a partner that is drug free. I'm not Mrs. Perfect, and I don't proclaim to be, nor do I claim to know it all. Perfection is just a word that helps you look from the inside of a person—it is the outer part that attracts a person to you but the inner part of the person is what keeps you around. I'm just a hard working, honest woman looking for someone special-basically a friend, first. At 57 years of age I definitely don't have time for games . . . . I have been hurt, therefore I truly know what that is like and in no way am I looking for revenge.

I like to travel, go for long drives on weekends, but basically I'm a homebody, I enjoy having friends over or just chilling out with someone socially. I'm not looking for a bed partner, (unless the chemistry over-flows—lol) nor do I need anyone to take care of me-I've been working since the age of 12 and still on the job) I'm just looking for a decent friend and companion. I would love to get to know you without a doubt. I'm ole school plus old-fashioned. I like to take time to know a person before I go there. If you are beginning to think I am gay, don't!!! I'm all woman, just not promiscuously like a lot of our women that are so easy, or desperate.

Sometimes God allows suffering in order to get our attention: to divert us from the wrong paths; to build our faith and our courage, to help us grow strong and

resilient; or to make us wiser. I say this because I feel the suffering from my divorce has made me stronger, wiser, and more resilient to the crooks and turns that our lives can take when least expected. Therefore; I need to know "What are you truly looking for in a partner?"

EJ, sometimes the honesty a person shows you upfront is what will keep a person around you for a lifetime!!! Many of our black brothers are looking only at the cover (the outer appearance of a woman) but we all have to be real . . . . most of us won't find that person we are looking for, if we all just look at the cover of a person without getting to know them (regardless of their race) or getting them to open up, we might have just passed our blessing . . . . (Just a thought from my mind to yours) May God bless you in your search if I'm not the one!!!!!*****Just wanted to let you know what is on my mind and how I think in terms of relationships today. The key component is communication, which most men duck and dodge. This is a quote:

"The Road to Success is not Straight. There is a Curve called Failure, a Loop called Confusion, Speed Bumps called Friends, red lights called Graves, Caution Lights called Family. You will have Flats called Jobs. But, if you have a Spare called Determination, an Engine called Perseverance, Insurance called Faith, and a Driver called Jesus, you will make it to a place called Success!

An old saying by my great grandmother, that was often repeated to us.

Sincerely, (BBarb) my pet name

My favorite music is down home blues, jazz, R&B and oldies to smooth the soul. Please, I am upfront and honest and you need to be also,

JUST KEEPIN IT REAL.

Life is always full of choices

No matter what happens to you,
or what ill advised events you go thru
You can always change your life by
making the right choices or positive choices
Being human and young as well as impressionable,
Sometimes we don't make the right choices.
Because you have a certain amount of Vulnerability
And you need tenacity to be able to let certain things go.
Your family and friends both act as care giving units
They provide continuing nurturing, love, and devotion.
Family and friends are the greatest reward in this world.
Because they always care for you without hesitation,
And they continue to love without any limitation.
Having a family give unconditional love without expectation
Will help you remember when you are without communication.
Listening is a wonderful blessing that gives us another start of
What life is about?
Making good choices can help you grow, make you happy
and become closer to the one you love and another.
If you show love and concern to your fellow man and brother.
(7/7/09)

What I'm Seeking in a Partner

First of all he needs to be charming fun and sensual.
Willing to share life with me like an equilateral
triangle.
And has the same feeling as I have.
He also needs to possess wisdom, intelligence and honesty.
And he should have a great sense of who he is.
I am looking for a man that can express himself to me romantically
everyday when the time comes.
I need a man that is willing to start out with me as a friend
with a genuine heart
and ready to have fun from the start.

Please no games! I've been there done that!
I am ready to share good times and great laughs.
Bottom line I would like to meet my best friend.
I have a lot of love to share with someone who is deserving.
I am tired of holding this love inside.
I sincerely need someone to love that I can't live without
Are you that friend?
Is there any men out there who are reliable and consistent?
I know it is, step Forward! I can be very irresistible!
I know that looks can catch anyone's eye
But true personality captures the heart.
To the world you maybe just one person
But to me you would be my world.

PART II

Poems of Unrequited Love, Love that Went Awry, and Trying to make a Connection

Barry

BARRY, Barry, Barry,
you came into my life so contrary,
Arrogant, very; but proclaiming to be the King of truth
Reassuring me with hope and aspiration that you were the one for me
By reciprocating your fathom of love with dozens of yellow and purple roses.
Yielding me to surrender as your yokemate,
but never fulfilling my empty heart
with concrete passion.

Bam
April 10, 2012

You Put a Smile on my face

Just like I was on drugs completely in a Daze
You put a smile on my face.
Looking for a man that will let me be the one on his mind
Waking up in each other arms
Melting all over again because he is not looking at the time.
A loving man is what I craze
So put a smile on my face.
I want a man that will let me put on his dress shirt or T shirt.
I want a man that will hold my pillow
Just to savor my scent when I am not home
A man that feels good when he is with his woman
And can show the world that he's happy and not alone.
I need a lovely man not going thru a phase
Come! Put a smile on my face.
I want everyday of our lives to be thoughtful and sweet
I want to be the sunshine in your windows when we meet.
Darling, let me be your black queen and you my black king
So we can thank the man upstairs for making you my everything.
So lets not let true love drift away
Put a smile on my face
And love me another day,

Are You The One I'm Looking For?

Cal, the more I hear from you,
the more I want to hear from you and get to know you
Someday I feel it would be nice to be with you and be
your girl.
I want us to become the most envied couple in the world.
So are you the one I'm looking for?
I want to have a relationship that will surpass the love affair
of Barack and Michelle Obama.
I'll like to wake up beside you everyday and fumble
Start your day off with nutrients of love and kisses.
Ending your night with many, tight hugs
And wakeup drinking coffee in just one mug.
Could you be the one I'm looking for?
I'll like to hold your hands every step we make
Because this is the kind of love I have been dreaming of
for years.
I'm hoping it can become a reality with out fears
And we can affectionately call one another "Boo".
Please can you be or are you the one
To make me blush
With love so strong that can turn my soul to mush
Could you be the Knight and shining armor I need
To fulfill my life
So I don't have to look no more
Because I see you walking through my door.

Written by Bam Jan 6, 2011

Darling Your Heart

Darling your heart will always be strong healthy and intact
    as long as you are with me.
I've never broken anyone's heart,
I've always been the receiver of the broken heart
      -getting my heart broken-
But over the years, I've learned how to be strong,
    I've learned how to pick up the broken pieces,
       and just move the hell on.

When I'm in a relationship,
I'm a very faithful person, but I will walk if I'm being cheated on,
      or taken for granted . . . .
Any man that gets involved with me should be fully aware
That I will not be taken for granted . . . . Ever Again!!!
Darling your heart will always be strong healthy and intact
      as long as you are with me.

I love communication in a relationship-
I don't like having a silent partner
    —that's not willing to talk or work things out,
Or put forth some effort in moving forward.
That's Why Darling your precious heart sing songs of cheer
      So have no fear!!!!
You can count on me, I will always be right here,
Darling your heart will always be strong healthy and intact
      as long as you are with me.

Dreaming Wonderful Dreams

As I lie here in my White Wrought Iron
Canopy bed,
Thinking sincerely how you live in my head,
I want to let you know, you are truly the yellow
sunshine of my life.
I truly hope that you will always be a round to keep me
romantically satisfied like a good spice,
I am dreaming wonderful dreams about you as my lover.
I am dreaming of you kissing me under the cover
And ending our nights with strong embraces,
While holding each other tight all night long
Please baby be the one to fulfill my life,
I hope to forever dream wonderful dreams about you and me
Dreams of you living in my head is where I want to be!

You keep me Uplifted

You are truly the missing piece of my life.
Your nurturing gives me the ultimate high
I truly hope that you will always be a round to keep me
Feeling Uplifted, loved, and supported,
So never say goodbye.
I am dreaming insatiable dreams about you as my forever
lover.
I want to wake up beside you morning, noon, and night
starting our day off with passionate embraces,
While building our love holding hands every little step we
take,
Because your superpowers keep me uplifted, loved and
supported.
I don't want to Look any more,
Anyone else would be an imposter, so don't ever walk
out the door.
I love the way you keep me feeling uplifted, loved and supported.

Fly, Fly Away Boy

I was minding my Biz
Walking to the (Dairy Queen) DQ to get a cold buz
 With my best friends, Drew, Perry, and Liz.
Suddenly, a gray Falcon Ford, graced my view.
I gasped, didn't know what to do.
Inside was a bunch of fine chocolate brothers.
 He was tall with thick lips like no other.
I said Fly, Fly away boy
 I'm no one's toy.

HE opened the car door
And hit the pavement floor
While keeping stride with me
I noticed he was (6'4") tall and handsome as could be.
He looked at me, I looked at him.
 And he said I'm Not like them.
I said Fly Boy, Fly, Fly away Boy
 I'm not your average female toy.

Keeping stride, he swaggered down the street.
 With his 6'4 frame stepping to a beat.
His walk was like the Prez, "That Barack Obama"
I thought, am I about to take a tumble.

As we approached the DQ, he beat me to the punch
 He quickly order a chocolate malt,
  And reached for his wally
Smiled at me and asked the clerk
  What's the tally?
I thought, Fly boy, Fly away from here
 Don't make me shed a tear!

Instead, he grabbed two straws and motioned me to sit.
The place was crowded and I didn't want to pitch a fit.
　　　So I sat across from him,
As he intently stared into my eyes with his mesmerizing
　　　Hazel peeps
Sending my body into a Transcendental sleep.
　　Fly Boy, FLY AWAY BOY
But my heart kept swelling like weight watchers Soy!

We finished our malt,
Sipping slowly while in deep thought.
　　I didn't want this moment to end.
But we were already sipping air from the bottom of the malt jar.
As the story was about to end—he said his name was "RW"
What's yours—before I could speak,
　　He asked, "Do you believe in Love at first sight?"
My goal is to love you with all my might,
　　And forever hold you tight.
　　　This story did not end
The romance was about to begin.
I was dumbfounded, I had no clue what to say or do
But if you want to know the rest of this continuing saga
　　　Stay tuned for Book Two
But in the meantime Fly, Fly Away Boy
　　You can't nurture me like a Matel TOY!!!!!!!!!

(This is the true Story of my First Love)

I Dreamt of My Boo!

Hello My Boo,
I dreamt of kissing your thick juicy lips
and touching your soft face.
In our own microcosm world in a very private place
Just the two of us you and me,
Loving each other without leaving a trace

Hello My Boo!
For me you have been like a new lease on life
Since we started our journey through this fairy tale land
Embracing each other so tight and squeezing each other's hand.
As we listen to a you and me band.
I want this journey to go on forever,
where the never-ending rivers flows.
As we trail blaze a path for all lovers to run,
Chasing their dreams as the billowry raging wind blows.

I love you

Sure baby, I Love you,
    Yes, I Do
I Love you
I can smell a very good lifetime with you
That thought alone can make me happy always and forever.
    Because I love you.
I am going to love you for who you are
And believe me always be there for you,
    Just don't hurt me!
Then we will always be happy . . .
    Because I love you
Sincerely I miss chatting on the phone with you
And hope you miss chatting with me too
    But I cant help it . . .
This is a test for our relationship.
    So don't forget me baby!
Because I Love you, I surely DOOOOOOO!.

Written
—On **Fri, 4/16/10, Barbara Murray** *<bambam2352002@yahoo.com>*

The Day I Fell In Love With You . . .

The Day I fell in Love with you
I can't tell you how excited I felt
Pumped up, mellow, and like an ice cube that never melt.
I thought of you night and Day
There was never a moment when my mind didn't sway.

The Day I fell in love with you
You were my major focus thought by thought.
While at work if I didn't hear from you
    I felt distraught
Your love keep me full and satlated
You are my dreams for craving
And always keeps me meditating

The Day I fell in love with you,
You were like a powerfood passionate and very fulfilling
Always there to satisfy my sensational needs
    With A love so incomprehensible
        So vivacious
    So exuding and unique,
        So whimsical and electrifying,
That not even the universe could control.
Because we have a story that could never be untold.

Barbara to RW

My Pledge of Love For You

Darling I have made a vow, to no one but you.
I pledge my love to forever be true
I will care for you and treat you right
I'll caress your face all through the night
I'll feed. Clothe and keep you warm
Lift you up when you are down and keep you strong.

Missing You

When you're not here with me day or night
Nothing in my Day seems to go right.
My life is so incomplete, I can barely sleep
My heart is lamented, sad and forlorned
My dreams are unrefined and very foolish
And this makes my soul and entire being ghoulish.
I am missing you

Without your presence I'm merely non-existence from day to day
I am totally and completely LOST!
My whole being without you falls into a boring way
Because Without you I will never ever find
Another love so complete, euphoric, and intense to give me
    That everlasting peace of mind

I miss your smile, your glowing intenslty, and your internal strength.
I miss the walks in the park. Chatting at the bus stop
Reciprocating our love by meeting Wednesday's at IHOP.
I want you in my life forever
I miss you like the twelfth of never.
I want our love to intensify each and every day
Calling, Emailing, Texting, relaxing.
Whatever it takes as long as our love keep maxing
And our romance does not stalemate in one place
Because I'll miss you and your loving embrace.
So as you can see you have the missing key to my heart
I want you to know that I'll forever miss you from the start.
    I'm missing you right now!
    Oh Hell, I just miss you dear.

I'll Catch you If You Fall

Go on and fall down, don't feel like a clown,
Because I'll forever be around
Go ahead and fall apart
I'll be here waiting when you start
I'll catch you right into these arms of mine
Go on, forget about her, your woes and all past loves
Go on and forget about what's right or wrong
I'll wipe your troubles away,
Understand, You can lay your head on my shoulder any day
So just cry, until all of your troubles just fade away.
Because I'll be here to catch you if you trip or fall.
So go ahead and fall right here in these flexible arms of mine

Don't fret   Don't fret,
Just let me eliminate your worries and fears
I want to Wipe away all your tears,
As long as you know that I'm near
So its ok, if you fall, my dear.
My arms will be opened W-I-D-E . . . .
To catch you if you fall That's because I'm right here!!
    !!!!!!!!!!!!!!!!!!!!!!!!!!!!!!!!!!

"Keeping the Faith In You"

I balance my life from almost every aspect
I balance my moods and emotions
I balance my beliefs and ideas
I even balance my dynamic life style with my ole fashion middle of the road ways
    of thinking
I balance the things you've said, and the things you haven't said, With what I believe
    are true,
I balance the true measures of your words and hold them close
to my Heart.
Because I balance, I keep the faith
I trust . . . that whatever happens between us is because we
understand one another.
My honesty . . . . are the feelings for you that I never want to hold
back
Peace . . . . Of mind is that you accept me for who I really am
and I accept you for who you are,
not something I want you to be.
Beauty . . . . is looking at more than just appearance, it's the
uniqueness of your style
It is the twinkling in your eye, and the crown of your smile
That makes me want to travel a mile
Just to spend time with you.
So I'm Keeping the faith in you.
I balance my life with freedom . . . freedom to be alone, free to be
myself, free to change and grow
Only if I know—
There is hope for me and you
The Chaos in this crazy world would never make me blue.
I'm Keeping the faith in you.
Joy . . . would be greeting you every day,
Savoring every memory of you in every way.
I would keep the faith if LOVE would come my way,
warm and secure

LOVE that would last a lifetime—perhaps far beyond
our heart and souls
That's only comparable to the essence of a bottle of fine wine,
as we grow old
Together, aging beautifully as ONE, just me, with just you and Time!!!!!!!!!!!! As I
    keep the Faith in with only you—all mine

Incomprehensible Love

You have a love so passionate and deep
A need so powerful and strong
A want so yielding and tantalizing
That the universe can't handle
Your love is one of a kind
That it blows my mind
It is a love so incomprehensible
And uniquely whimsical.

Your love is so rapturous and jubilant
It puts me in seventh heaven
I love you today,
I will love you tomorrow and forever
I will love you every day and every night
I will always yarn to hold you tight.
I will love you unconditionally
Because your love is so exhilarating and incomprehensible,
Yes, incomprehensible, incomprehensible and blissful
It is like resting my body and soul in God's Paradise.

Drowning In Your Love

Its three o'clock in the morning
I have been tossing and turning all night long.
Visions of your kissable lips and outreached arms is where I belong
Thoughts of you are overwhelming my senses
I'm drowning in your love
No matter what I do, I can't seem to rise above.

I woke up this morning dreaming I was stroking your face
I reached for your body
But there was no trace
I sat up in my canopy bed
Visible shaking my head
I can't get a grip
Because I'm drowning in your love
No matter what I do,
I can't seem to rise above
This wonderful feeling when I dream of you!!!

PART III

Questioning it All! Does True Love Really Exist?

Questioning It All!
Is true love real, or can it be found?

Thursday, Jan.6th, 2012 3:26 AM

Poem—Questioning It All

Hope you like—It's just because I love to write and create my thoughts into poetry-It fills the void in my life and gives me a completeness. Not meant to be obtrusive! And also I hope it does not offend you but it was my true feelings at the moment.

Questioning God or Questioning it All?

When I think of you
And how you barraged into my life
Did God send you as the one I was looking for
Yes, that outgoing, energetic, good-looking, gorgeous lipped, romantic man that
    believes he could Perhaps, be
My one and only
    True love that is,
Or could you be that true love for every woman you meet
    on the BPM or cyber-sites

I believe there is a true love for everyone on the universe
For God has given every man a time for change
Could God have sent you to be the keeper of my soul?
Or perhaps he sent you as the strength in my sprints.

Is True Love Real or Can It Be Found?

Is True Love Real or Can It Be Found?
True Love, What is it? Where is it?
True love can't be bought
Or just sought.
True Love, Yes, I'm talking about True Love,
Can it be found,
Searching from the Ground!
Many have fallen in and out of love while searching
for their one and only true love.
True love is real but it can't be found.
Please stop wasting your time looking around.
The greatest example of True Love was given to us
from the good Lord above.
"For God so loved the world that he gave his only begotten
Son, that whosoever believe in him shall not perish
but have everlasting life"
True Love is not something you find,
It is something you give.
If "to give" is not your intention, then I must say
you have the wrong woman, I'm not the
Mrs. Right for YOU!!!!!!

Can anything be more beautiful than this feeling

Can anything be more beautiful than this feeling
When I think of you a little pucker plays on my lips,
Like receiving a million dollars for a tip.

A strange glow of sheer happiness refuses to leave my
heart.
OH! What a divine gift of love you gave from the
start.

Baby this happens every time you come to mind.
If this is love, then I love the feeling of being in love with you!

The sound of your voice, sends shivers up my spine
The affixation of Compassion in your embrace.
Is sometimes troubling, like losing a marathon race.
The serenity in your stride like Barack Obama
    Makes my heart somersault and rumble

When you walk across a room
I feel the most empowering Boom!.
If this is love, then I love the feeling of being in love with you!

The beating of your heart rejoices my soul
Like the ending of a fairy tale that's never been told.
Your promise of tomorrow, That we WILL never part.
Is Heavens' declaration of a dedicated heart.
If this is Love I love the Feeling of being in love with you!!!

Can anything be more beautiful than this feeling I have for you!
Because I love the feeling of being in love with you too.
The beauty of your kiss, and that magic In your touch.
Is for all these reasons and more,
    That I simply love you so much!!!!!!!!!!

Could God have sent you with all your messages

Could God have sent you with all your messages
phone calls, and simple flirts,
       Just to get under my skirt?
Could God have sent you? Yes I question it all?
Did he send you to travel beside me
As a special companion
Did he send you to ride my bike with, or take long drives,
Or take a long walk through Cadwalder Park
As I write poetry, laying my head on your chest
And listen to your heart bark

Yes, I question it all. So am I questioning God?
Or am I questioning you!
Perhaps, Because I don't believe in playing games
So don't bring them.
I am looking for my soul mate
Not just someone that wants to play Patty Kate
I am looking for
My forever love, my heart, my partner in life, my joy
But never a toy boy.
Could God have sent you? Yes I question it all?

I am looking for that Special man
Someone that does not mind a woman
    that wants to pamper him as a King
And be his Queen for as long as God gives us life
Someone that will share Love in truth
As God has given it in depth
Let's make it deeper than the love God has given to man
For with his blessings I will not settle for less
Than love at its the best.
So, Could God have sent you with all your messages?
      Yes I question it all?

Is This Love?

When I think of you I think of the most beautiful flowers on the planet
Red Roses, Purple Lilies, pink pansies and yellow lilacs
Is it true love I feel for you
I think of you in everything I do.
My enthusiasm and passion for you is like a Godly joy
Like the fulfillment of a kid with his favorite toy.

Within every beat of my heart there is a feeling of happiness
Floating inside like a puffy white cloud
This feeling happens every time you cross my mind.
Is this Love I'm feeling, Or a waste of time

Can the illuminating smile on my face cultivate the fruit of Love?
Especially when your lips touch mine
locked as we embrace.
Could this be Love? A perfect bond of union
Stinging my soul like a smelly onion
Your sweet breath breathing on my neck cause me to quiver and shiver within.
Just the touch of your hand
is like a Michael Jackson song without a band
The smell of your hair
has the sweet aroma of a Chinese Pear
This feeling of happiness refuse to leave my heart.
This happens each time we are apart.

Correct me If I am Wrong

Correct me if I am wrong
We spent hours talking on the phone
But the lies you tell is like keeping the beat to a song
You said you didn't know Lucy Wong
But yet I caught you hiding her pink thong

Correct me if I am wrong
You think I'm weak, but I am woman that's strong
Last night when I asked if you were home
You said you were all alone
To tell lies like that is a simply wrong
Because it is not cool being a player trying to belong.

Correct me if I am wrong
You said I looked pretty in my green Sarong
But you were trying to appease me by trying to get along
Trying to be with you I won't prolong
So Lose my number because I m not a tag-a-long.

Created: 2:07 a.m. 9/2/13

If You Love Yourself

Ladies if you love yourself
And I know you do
Never ever GIVE MORE OF YOURSELF
Than YOU GET IN RETURN.
Many men can be weeded OUT QUITE EASILY
Based on their INTENTIONS AND their MOTIVES,
BUT YOU MUST PLAY A ROLE IN IT Too
BY KEEPING YOUR HEART in your chest longer) and your panties up around your waist
Or UNTIL HIS HEART IS IN IT OR AT LEAST GOING Toward your WAY.
MEN OPERATE more toward the PHYSICAL
Whereas we as women are more emotional than mental
So my friends DO IT THE RIGHT WAY, MENTALLY,
PUT HIM TO THE TEST FIRST
AND SEE IF HE PASSES.
THE MOST IMPORTANT THING A WOMAN CAN GIVE A MAN
IS HER HEART first not opened Legs
SO WHAT IS HE bringing to the table
Is it Nothing but more than wonderful NIGHTS OF MAD PASSIONATE LOVE
AND DAYS OF HELL to pay later
While KEEPing HIS HEART TO HIMSELF
BECAUSE HE ALREADY HAS YOUR'S
My Sisters, we need to know that THE WAY TO A MAN'S HEART IS NOT THROUGH
    your PRIVATE PARTS
BUT THROUGH your MIND AND SOUL First.
Ladies if you love your self,
Then ONLY YOU CAN SHOW a man that you love yourself, by making your body a
    sacred shrine that God meant it to be.
Don't be too eager to please a brother by letting him savor the essence of your
    fruits on his terms.
Maya Angelou feels "The beauty of a phenomenal woman is not what others see
    in her, but what she sees in herself".
No matter how sexy you are, IF YOU COULD TRULY LOVE SOMEONE FOR JUST
    ONE NIGHT Do it WITH ALL YOUR HEART and all you might.
Do it first, mentally not the physical.
THAT PERSON SHOULD BE YOU,
THEN OF COURSE, the man, hopefully someone
Wh0's deserving of such a beautiful creature like you!!!!!

PART IV

If You Dwell on Yesterday, Tomorrow may Never Come or be Visualized

If you dwell in Yesterday, Tomorrow may never be visualized

If you dwell on what happened in yesterday,
Today may not be realized and tomorrow never visualized . . . .
So let's just make up now,
Let by gones—be—by gones
Yeah, I know you believe in sharing
As well as being loving and caring
So lets not worry about what happen yesterday
Or the day before
Because love has no distance but lust does
You are in Afghanistan and I'm in New Jersey,
No matter where you are,
I only know I can't live without you
The reality of it all is no one knows what tomorrow will bring
But if we bask in today our two hearts can sing!!!
So don't live for the past, if you want our love to last.
Dwelling on what happened yesterday, today may not be realized
     and our tomorrows never visualized.

If I Could Freeze Time

If I could freeze time and make it stand still,
I would freeze it right here,
So you'd always hold me, closer and near.
In your arms is where I want to be,

Filled with the timeless impeccable love you've given me.
If I could freeze Time and make it turn blue
I would put a bond on it so strong
    and hold you like crazy glue.
To know you're the one; my 'Mr. Right'.
You are a blessing sent from up above,
The world should know we have found our true love.

If I could freeze time and make it stand still
I would entertwined and mold our lives as one,
And keep our love shining as bright as the sun.
You and I will find nothing less,
Than eternal love and everlasting bliss.

My Life, My Passions

My Life, My Passion and Why You?

Hi Mr. R,

How are you? I do hope fine? Since I express myself better in writing than any other form I am going to attempt to make you see my true meaning of what's important to me in life. As of now, First, my daughter, my new son-in-law and my new granddaughter, are the most significant in my life right now other than my loving and caring family. Out side of that there is no connection to anyone or a significant other. NO ONE or nothing else except my career, which is about to come to a close.

Why You?

Then on March 13, 2011, I opened my mail from **BPM** after being away at a conference for a week end with my friend in Television. That's when I came across you and your first message, It was something about you that caught my eye. Maturity, that is something that I thought we both had, Then you seemed like such an honest, intelligent, nurturing person., which is my personality also.

I read your profile over and over before I responded because I wanted to make sure we had a lot in common. After talking with you, I discovered such beautiful demeanor in your voice, and I guess being vulnerable and away from men over the past 5 years, like a teenager's dream I let my guard down and allowed my self to start falling for you. Probably deeper than I realized. So now you have it.

I am an ambitious person that always set goals for myself to reach by a certain time. Since I'm retired with leisure time to accommodate someone in my life, its ironic how you actually fell right into that time frame. I had asked God to send someone, loving, kind, supportive, and romantic into my life by my 60th birthday so I could start dating again. And every time I looked up, there you were with one beautiful inspiring message after the other, and most of all those unspeakable lips, that's hard to reject for a woman like me that has a lip fetish. My grandmother would also tell us girls that the world is a playground, which could be negative or positive. But by putting God first in your life makes the positive occur within, because entering a relationship with just the negatives you will surely be played.

My Passion—If I want it I'm Passionate about it!!!

So **Mr. R**, the negative is not what I'm looking for. Baby, I'm very passionate about everything I do in life. I'm passionate about my career as well as the men in my life. I don't take on any project or anything unless I'm passionate about it. I have a short attention span, therefore; I have to be passionate or it wouldn't work. Things I'm passionate about I will devote my time 24-7, or work around the clock to see the finished product.

Yes, I have an attraction to you, but you would not be in my mind or my thoughts this long if I weren't passionate about you. Whatever I'm passionate about I will move mountains and jump hurdles to make it work. That's because I'm just that ambitious. So I just wanted to make that very CLEAR!!! I'm not getting any younger and I'm getting ready to retire, therefore; I'll like to have someone there to reach out to, to talk to, and to travel with, someone whenever I can

I love to hold hands and look my partner straight in the eyes. I will also like to know that they got my back because I certainly will have theirs. You showed so much inspiration and intent from the beginning or maybe I am misinterpreting that you wanted the same quest for life as I do. (Am I wrong **Mr. R**—please just stop me if you have no interest in me moving toward building a greater friendship and hopefully something we both would be pleased and happy with in the future. Stop me!! now and I will move on). I have a crush on you and I'm not afraid at all to let you know that, So if my thinking is wrong, and your motives are something else-or some place else for that matter, you are a man and I will understand.

After all I grew up with 14 males in my life constantly, I have (5) brothers and (9) first cousins so its like having 14 brothers. There is more to you than meet the eye. There are worldly things that you know that not many people know. You are so wise and intelligent beyond your years dear and I know that for a fact. My initial impression of you is that you are a pretty serious guy. So am I.

I think you and I both live in our own micrcosm world. I can tell that you have a world of your own where you escape to every now and then. It is there you find inner peace. (Same here). You are able to block out what you don't need and encourage what you believe you need. You are a very careful person and so am I, but the great thing about me is that I never give up. So I am still preparing for and getting ready to bring that special person into my life and my world. Since I think we have the chemistry and the attraction for one another, why not give it a try?

Are You prepared and willing to take a chance on me Mr. R? In mean in the manner as your partner. I sense you are very aware of the fact that I am a few years older than you, but being the person that I am and if FATE brings you in my life and my world I would certainly bring you maturity, understanding, love, peace, joy, generosity, patience etc. I sense your integrity. I sense your longing to be at peace with yourself and I sense you are not into the physical, you are more into the mental, emotional, the spiritual, and all other aspects that are conducive to growth and fulfilling your goals and that's what makes us compatible baby.

I'm not asking for your hand in a marriage-not ready,

I not looking for anyone to take care or keep me-God gave me that gift of blessings to help myself.

I'm not looking for someone to give me a brand new car—I have one,

I'm not looking for high maintenance and diamond rings—not my lifestyle, I'm a plain Jane.

I'm not looking for someone that will run around and cheat—because I don't cheat in a relationship.

I'm looking for that SPECIAL SOMEONE to be supportive, loving, kind, to rebuild my psyche, a shoulder to lean on, a kick-in-the-pants when I need help to get through confusing moments and painful times, someone to share the good news and bad news. Someone to forgive and forget, and makeup like tomorrow is never coming, someone to fill the lonely hours, someone to remember thoughts I've been trying to forget, someone to express anger in a positive way, and not take my kindness for weakness., and someone to disassociate me with the other women that caused turbulent for you. I need that Special Someone to realize that I can only be Me, and you can only be you; but if by chance we can bring happiness to one another. **Let's embark!**

I do hope this is clear and precise—Can you take a chance on me? All you have to do is send me a YES OR NO in my email. So I can move on baby.

Enjoying my Life at Age 62

AS The Leaves Are Falling Down,
I'm so thankful to still be around
For Another Year to enjoy Wonderful Family and Friendship!
Join Me in the Celebration for my 62nd Birthday
Seeing all my loved ones is always an inspiration
Your strength brightens my day
And keeps me rolling along the way
My life is always challenging and changing
For the Best that is,
I've had my trials, tribulations, up and downs,
But it so important to know that my close knit family is around
So join me in celebrating this new milestone
At age 62, I have now reached my comfort zone!

PART V

Take Me To The Next Phase, Keeping It REAL!!!

Communication Means

It's amazing that I know how to communicate to you.
But you must know how to communicate with me.
Express your feelings and your emotional short comings.
I should not have to second guess anything.
Because we should be on the same page
Our thoughts and revelations should be insinc.
Questions should be asked by both partners,
Without hesitation in a gentle and calming manner.
Miscommunication leads to misunderstanding and misinterpretation.
One partner cannot say I'm sorry and the other remain silent
Both parties should end up saying I'm sorry and trying to work things
out.
Communication means to speak out, not shout

Keeping It Real Is My Name

I would say keeping it real is my name,

Communication is my game and the key to making me happy. Finding some one to give my heart to is what I am after . . .

SO CAN YOU PLEASE MEET ME HALFWAY . . .

I'm looking for . . . A true friend,

> That's got it together with the aim to making me smiling and keeping me happy with him as a life partner.

> Wanting me for me Accepting the good and the bad And growing as one heart beat . . . can you handle that . . . come get me.

> I'd just like to add . . .

Life is made for us so lets handle it.

and if you don't know what you want please pass me by . . . I am looking for the real man that knows himself and wants

to know his woman . . . ~me~

Just need someone nice to show me,

Cause keeping it REAL is my name.

I'm a Special Kind of Woman

I'm a special kind of woman,
Are you a special kind of man?
I'm wondering who you thought you were
Sending me flirt after flirt
Somehow I knew I had to get a grip
So I would not get hurt.

Once in a while I think about how good
I know we could be
And then you don't call-which cause me to doubt
Wondering if you feel the same about me
I know that I'm a special kind of woman.
Ambitious, amicable, honest,
Hardworking, independent, and always
Self sufficient.
At this time I want to know if you feel like I do
Or do you care for me too.
I'm walking around with my heart in my hand,
Wondering if I should just give the hell up
Because true Love doesn't exist on this land

Are You that Special Kind of Man?

Once in a while I want you to understand
That you always put a smile on my face
That no storm, cloud, or rain can replace.
You made my heart take wings
I'm flying around curvafused,
Because you are weighing heavily on my mind
Like flowers blooming from an April RAIN
I think about how good I know we could be
Then you take me off track and . . .
Make me wonder if you feel the same about me
Yes, I'm walking around with my heart in my hand
When you came along—something happened
I let my 60 foot gate down
and you ended up in my town.
Perhaps it's why I'm a special kind of woman
And you are that special kind of man.
I made up my mind—out of 500 hits and flirts on bpm
About 321 don't meet my age criteria
143 either not my type or don't respect woman severely.
And the other 46 have possibilities or prospective maybes
But don't have your Golden Boy image, your rich Carmel color,
Your enriched temperate personality,
And every woman's dream, your delectable thick lips,
Your Rockmond Dunbar body, as well as your
Raw and uncut sexy voice
Wondering if I should just give up—NO That's why I chose you.
I feel that You are that Special Kind of Man

Barbara—RAW AND UNCUT 5/9/2011

Thanks For Being You!

Thanks for Everything-Thanks for being my one in a Million!!!!!!!!!!!!!!!!

Thanks for being you . . . .
For being there for me . . . . For caring about me . . . .
For being my greatest best friend and
maybe someday my one and only man????
Thanks for letting me into your heart . . . . And for being gentle with my heart
Thanks for understanding me . . . . For accepting me as I am . . . .
And the way that I am
Thanks for making me smile, no matter how I feel
Thanks For standing beside me and not in front of me
Thanks for supporting me . . . .
For seeing me the way you do . . . .
Thanks for not trying to change me . . . .
And for not being mad When I call or wake you up at all hours of the night . . . .
Just because I need to hear your voice
Thanks for making me feel like I'm everything . . . .
Thanks for all the little things you do that makes me feel like a statuette ten feet tall
When I am only five feet one inch . . . .
Thanks for loving my annoying little habits . . .
and For making me see how you see me . . . .
Thanks for encouraging me to do the things that I enjoy . . . .
And for accepting my beliefs instead of trying to change them . . .
Thank for not letting me take life too seriously and helping me to relax
Even when I'm stressing myself,
Barbara, thank you
Thanks For Everything . . . . for being my one in a million.
Always and forever yours

You Sent My Mind Winding Around a Curve

You broke the camels back when you sent me 8 messages in one day
Were you just Trying to get a play??????????
I thought that took nerve
Because you sent my mind winding around a curve.

My youthful heart can love you and give you what you need
But I'm too old to go chasing you—
So say exactly what you mean.
so you got to just give me

Give me one reason to let me know you are playing no game
That will rip my heart out and leave me lame
You see, its all your fault-
You got a lot of nerve
Sending me all your Castaways
As you sent my mind winding around a curve.

I didn't know if I should believe you—or just walk away
But I'm glad I stayed
Even though I got played.
Because you sent my mind winding around a curve . . . .

I Have Been Waiting

I have been waiting for a long time
And saving myself for the one that I know
That might be that special one
To make me feel good again
Along came you with a swagger
That makes my heart skips a beat
Somehow, everything happened so fast
My, I think we are going to last.
I think our friendship is going, gone beyond??????
I have been waiting
Gee, is this wait over?

I Have Been Waiting

I have been waiting
I have been waiting
Patiently,
Happily,
Sincerely,
Really, Really, waiting
I've come to the conclusion
We are not getting any younger
Gosh-Darn, if your love is real
Either marry me or walk away from love.

PART VI

Poetic Thoughts of Dedications and Bereavements to family and friends

My Heroes

My Heroes are my 5 brothers
They are superbly like no other.
Eddie. Ray, Milton, Robert, and June.
Are Brothers that are family oriented and in tune.
They are serious, wonderful, forgiving, and handy.
Each serving our country with pride and doing numerous tours of duty
You're Men of character that's absolutely dandy.
(special tribute to my five wonderful brothers)

God gave you the Gift of Love

Lady Gaines-When we first met those years 33 years ago,
I fell in love so fast, I knew right then,
You were the one and only one for me;
I knew I'd never have to look for love again.
Each anniversary finds us happier; Because God gave us the gift of love
You are my light—my moon, my star, my sun.
You show me what real love is all about,
You fill my life with pleasure, joy and fun.
As time goes by, your love grows stronger and stronger still.
Because You're the most amazing woman I know.

Bishop Gaines—You're Always been There for Me
When my world comes crashing in,
I turn my heart to you, and the Lord,
And pure, sweet peace I find.
Especially when chaos tries to rules my mind
Just like a drug You comfort me in pain;
You lift me out of trouble, You nourish, heal and cleanse me,
Like a cool refreshing rain.
In times of joy and bliss,
When things are going right,
You lift me even higher,
And fill me with delight.
You listen to my prayers;
You hear my every plea;
I'm safer because I know
You're always here for me
Today is A special world for you and me
Our anniversary means a lot,
You mean Much more to me today than any other day;
I celebrate my love for you,
And cherish you in every way.
Our life together gets better and better,
And I keep on loving you more and more.

We have a special bond that many people cannot see
It wraps us up in our own little cocoon
and God holds us fiercely in his womb
By binding us closer and keeping us strong

In his special world where he lifts us up to where we belong

Because GOD GAVE US THIS GIFT TO LOVE
IT IS UP TO US HOW WE USE IT.
SO LET'S keep the sunshine in the windows so,
GOD'S GIFT OF LOVE will not DRIFTING AWAY
Bishop and Lady Gaines your 30 year anniversary brings to mind
the happiness and joy you've brought to each other
The sweet memories, devoted love, laughter and also the tears
Have Given you peace, ecstasy to embrace the chaos and fears.
To cope with the ups and downs that life brings.
Because God gave you both the gift of Love.
To wake up each morning
And to look at each other and still get a thrill
Because your bond in marriage is the best thing in my life
And I can see that you love deeply and I hope you always will.
(Anniversary dedication of 33 years to Dr. Sidney and Lady Gaines)

Sophia

Sophia, You are like an angel that flew down to Earth.
You brought our family so much joy at the time of your birth.
One look in your bright eyes, none of us were ever the same.
Because you became a living doll each time we called your name.
There is a part in my heart and a bond that won't ever sever,
Sophia, you are our baby, our angel, and I'm sure along with your mom,
dad, grandpa, and grandma's, uncles and aunts, nieces, and nephews as
well as your favorite cousin kenzie and others we will all love and support you forever!
Sophia, you are more perfect than I could have hoped, your personality is
more beautiful than we ever dreamed.
Each day you are more precious that anyone could have imagined,
That's why I love you more than I could have ever
Known . . . .

(Created by Glam-ma Barbara for my only grandchild)

Here I Stand

(Dedicated to the families of Trayvon Martin and Rodney King)

Here I Stand
    With opened arms
What can I do?
To help you!
Here I stand
    To help bridge my people in this land.

Here I Stand
    Encourage me,
        Embrace Me,
Nurture me,
Help me become the best I can
    Open platform is where I take my stand
Here I stand
    To offer a helping Hand.

Here I Stand
    What's on your mind?
Tell me, Do you care?
    Enough to share,
        Do you know how to show love
    So outreach your arms
By reaching above,
Here I stand
    Like a one woman band
Ready to lift up all races of colors
    To help the causes of Trayvon Martin and Rodney King
And to seek refuge for all God's people.
Here I stand,
A woman but Bolder than any man.

Here I stand
    With opened arms
Can you spare a moment
    To Take a look
        Or just read a book
To take an impovished child off the hook
Here I stand
    Among the best kings and queens
        To take a stand when needed between.

For my Daughter I would

Tisa, for you I would climb
Mt. Everest highest peak
Swim the depth of the Pacific ocean
To capture the love of a daughter so meek.

Baby, for you I would crown you queen
And place upon your head the biggest crown
To fulfill a smile that's a mile wide
Just to know that you will always be by my side.

You are a daughter, O' so beautiful
Giving birth to you was a radical experience.
The moment the nurse place you in my arms
Your eyes lit up like a luminous light,
We could tell then that you would be ever so bright.
I pray that you never take your love away
For I reassure I love you every day
For you I would . . .
If I could
Make you the one
Who makes me whole
Because your birth captured my heart and touched my soul

Love Can Bred Love To Love

Hug me!
Embrace me!
Help me!
Love me!
Don't hate,
It's a tragedy.
Don't seek to crucify
    Make an effort to Defy
The ills of tomorrow
Love can Bred love
    To love others

Kindness!
Compassionate!
Giving,
Seeking,
Receiving,
Helping and sharing,
Love can bred Love to care

    Walk with me,
Talk with me
Be the one to reach out
     Remind yourself to
    Preach what Love is all About!
Never forget that Love can bred love
      to love

(Dedicated to the children of Haiti and other natural disasters)

Ernie, I Miss You

Ernie, I love you so much and I wish you were home,
It hurts me to think you're so alone.
Its not the same without you here,
Why you left so soon is still unclear.
Ernie, I miss You

Ernie, You were my big brother,

My best friend, and we were always together . . . .

Talking on the phone, going to doctor appointments
I will always love you no matter how long its been,
My love carried you until the day your life came to an end.
Ernie, *I miss my you, really I do*
When we were young I followed you,

We played, we fought, and had fun time too.

But as we grew older, You thought you knew it all,
As you rode your motorcycle and stuck you chest out
You appeared taller and bolder
I am so proud to call you my big brother
You stood by me and you protected me like no other,
When you died a part of my soul died with you. I loved you with all my might.
You will always be here in my heart
As I squeezed my pillow and think you each night.

(Dedication to my best friend-Dianne McCormick)

Arthur, You are Missed dearly

You were my big brother,
And I'll treasure you forever.

Arthur, You were my big brother, my best friend,
and we were always thick as thieves.
Talking on the phone, or going to South Carolina
Fishing on the banks of the Delaware River
Even when the days were so cold, I would quiver.
I will always love you no matter how long its been,

I miss you Arthur.

Arthur, I love you and I wish you were home,
Its not the same without you here,
Everyday I sit on the porch in my rocking chair wishing you were here . . . .
Each time we departed you said "See you later"
"I promise I'll be back my little alligator."
Of all the fun times you had promised to return whenever you left, filled my head
As we bid . . . farewell, *its hard to believe you are dead.*

Every morning as I wake up I think of you, as the hero that came into my life,
I am afraid I can not live without you
It hurts so much you never let me down, I just don't know what to DO!!!!!!

Dedicated to my Sister-in-Law, Viola Whalen

Gerald Deleon Bullard, A Gift of Love

Gerald, affectionately known as Jerry was a brother shared by
Gods Gift of Love
Over, beyond and above.
Like most people fall was his favorite time of the year
Enjoying family reunions with family and friends
While spreading good cheer
Gerald was kind and polite, even to strangers.
He tried to help others as much as he could.
Now his happiness dwell in the house of the Lord throughout the land,
as he prepares to greet and meet
his Grandma Dora, Aunt Marjorie, brother James, Lynn, and Larry.
Could this have been his master plan.
Gerald was a man of peace,
It was his dream that all fighting and strife would cease.
He shared a great love for others.
But his deepest love was the way he treasured his brothers and mother.
Love and peace to all my family in his absence.
You will truly be missed!

To my dear sister in Christ and best friend
Gale S. Bruner
Thanks for the memories of your Legacy. You were blessed to
retire from a career you truly loved, teaching, for 42 years.
You will forever be cherished as a sister, friend, colleague, mentor, teacher,
devoted wife and mother. Whenever something had to be done, I can still hear
you saying "Come on! Lets get it together, We can do this!" We loved you dearly
But God wants you to mentor and direct his Gym in heaven.
Forever and Always I will love you till eternity.
BAM

A Special Tribute to the Greatest Role Model

The Late Gale Bruner was the most impressive
And successful human Being I've known
At the end of her journey she globally traveled the world
To every corner of the earth planes have flown.
Gale Bruner had a smile that lit up the world
She was a woman that knew how to host with most
She found peace at the end of the day
When she would modestly brag or boast.
Whatever Gale did, she did it big time
Her accomplishments are memories forever embraced in her shrine
Gale was fierce, Oh! So fierce that her peers called it a crime
Because she was the greatest role model of all time.
Gale was a woman of honesty, integrity and determination
She would give you her two cents without hesitation
Her goal in life was to uplift, inspire, and encourage you to do more
Being true to herself was her legacy
She gave with her heart and shared it with me.
So when God called her home, he set her free.
Although her time expired so soon, was beyond her control
Having the strength to motivate others, showed us she was so bold!
We all should be grateful for Gale's love
As she looks down on us from heaven above.
Gale Bruner was truly a role model
With sheer determination, as she would address
her students as child or honey
The work she did for students, family, and friends
was for love, never money.
Hard work is what Gale brought to the table as a dance advisor,
student government advisor, cheerleading coach, Athletic director,
Teacher of the year, wife of Raymond and a great mother
The way she reached out to students and colleagues,
there will never be another
Because she was the greatest Role Model.

Forethoughts

It is my aspiration and complete elucidation that everyone who reads this book is able to gain reconciliation, reconnection, reminiscence, remembrance, or reflection on something or someone from a past or current relationship.

Hopefully, if you came across just one poem that stood out in your mind, then my contributions in this book have been visualized. If you found a specific poem that motivated you to make a connection I hope your dream are realized.

Poetic Thoughts in the keys of happiness is a feel good book of poems and poetic readings all about events of disbelief, unfairness, inspiration, separation, excitement, Love at first, reminiscence, healing, encouragement, and making connections THAT BROUGHT ABOUT ARBRITRARY EMOTIONS IN MY LIFE. It is a book that will ensure positive thinking and to also expound words of wisdom to help you become aware of the reasons people enter your life. Some may have great intentions and then there is always the chance of some just being there unwarranted.

Life is full of choices is a poem all about making positive choices that give us inner peace first and not about being persuaded to please others before pleasing ourselves. So parents, instill in your children to always stand for something and to make the right choices even if others may not agree with them.

Poems of dedications are to my siblings, my heroes (brothers), my child and my only grandchild. It is a validation of love for my family. I treasure my entire family to the utmost. They mean the world to me and vise versa. "Correct me If I Am Wrong" is a poem taking on men that I call "Lying Appeasers" or "Love scammers". The poem exposes vindictiveness for game players, and sugar daddies, that dwell on lying, being deceitful, lusting and cheating while in more than one relationship.

Sophia is the grandiose welcome of my first and only grandchild and the joy her birth brought to all paternal and maternal families. Sophia is like a living doll, she smiles, claps, dances and communicate with you in every aspect. Her personality is just raw, uncut, and unimaginable . . . **"Here I Stand"** was written in church as the choir was singing "Break Every Chain." This is a very powerful Gospel song. The poem is dedicated to the families of Trayvon Martin and Rodney King.

It is my hope that our Legal Justice system will one **day** rise above racism and prejudice against various races and hear the chains of injustice falling link-by-link—and the breaking of each link will restore the wrongs that have been done to all God's people .

"God Gave us the Gift To Love" is all about showing alliance to love the one you are with and family.

It is based on the relationship of a wonderful couple that has been married and pasturing together for over 33 years. They love god and adores one another. I wrote the poem based on the passionate appreciations and contributions they exhibit to the world in their daily relationship. Their relationship gives leeway that a good woman or a good man is not hard to find, it is how you treat and respect each other once you find them. The poem is based on my interpretation of the support, joy, and pleasure they receive from helping one another in their daily lives as well.

My advice to everyone is to rethink any issues you have with your family and express your gift to love and understanding . . . A good relationship with family and friends is paramount. Counselor Mark Bryan stated that "If you can decode your family messages of love and affection from the past and from today, then you can open the door to richer family ties."(Mark Bryan, Codes of Love, Pocket Books, 1999)

It is my hope that this book provides something "Special" for everyone that reads it. Sincerely Barbara (aka, BAM)

List Of Author's Credentials

Education

MBA program at Grand Canyon University, in Phoenix, Arizona, enrolled for degree in Administration and Principal Ship. (awaiting to return after being sidelined by an auto accident.)
Master of Education, Curriculum Design and Technology—Houston Baptist University, Houston Texas 5/2002.
ECC, Princeton , NJ-PowerPoint Technology Training—August 2000
MBA Program—Urban Education, William Paterson University, Wayne, NJ 5/83 (Honors)
Bachelors of Art—Elementary Education, Rider University, Lawrenceville, NJ, 2/79
Associate of Arts Degree with Honors, Mercer County Community College, Trenton, NJ; 6 /76 (Dean's List)

Teaching Employment—Trenton Board of Education—1979—2011

P J Hill Elementary School, 2009-2011 2nd Grade
Robbins Annex—2007-2008—4th grade
Carol Robbins Elementary School—2006-2007—4th Grade
Floating Replacement Teacher—for all Grade Levels K-12 ; 2005-2006
Grant Elementary School—1985-2005—4th, 5th, and 6th Grades
Patton J Hill Elementary School-1979-1985-4th & 5$^{th \ Grades}$,

Seminar Workshops and Professional Training

National Writers' Institute's Program-Rider University-Summer, 2010,

NCTM—National Conferences of Teachers of Math—5-Day Conference, April 2002
     Las Vegas, NV
NCTM—Math Academy—5 Day Training, April 2001
     Orlando, Florida
NCTM—National Conference of Teachers of Math—April 6-11, 2001
     Orlando, Florida

LSS—Laboratory for Students Success—3 Day Conference—November 2000
       Washington D.C.
NCTM—Math Conferences of Math Teachers—April 2000
       Chicago, Illinois
Science Ambassador-Liberty Science Center—Workshops, 1998-2001
       Jersey City, NJ (Grant School).
Princeton University—Princeton Plasma & Physic Lab—Summer Lab—37 Hours
       Princeton, New Jersey July 13th-17th 1998
Quest—Teachers Preparation Program—Princeton University—(Attended (3) Summers)
       Princeton, New Jersey—1991, 1995, & 1997
Denver OIC—Keypunch & Data Processing ,1972
       Denver, Colorado
McKinney Job Corp—Certification—Retail Sales & Drapery-making , 1969-1971
       McKinney, Texas

Award Nominations—Nominated by FBBA as an Outstanding Educator and Community Leader—2010
Nominated and selected winner of National Liberty History Museum—Hero Teacher of the Year—2009
Nominated—N J Governor Teacher of the Year—I995-Gov. Christie Whitman
Nominated—NJ Teacher of the Year—2000
Nominated—Who's Who Among American Educators, 1983, 1996, 1999, 2003
Outstanding Teacher of the Year—I982
Listed in the National Registry of outstanding Teachers in America—Network Directory For Who's Who in Education—2007

PROFESSIONAL ASSOCIATION MEMBERSHIP AND CITATIONS

Member of (NCTM) **National Conference for Teachers of Mathematics** 1999-2006
Benjamin Banneker Association—National Chapter—Attend National Meeting 1999-2002
NAACP-National Advancement Association for Colored People
Member and avid supporter
Parent Support Team—Grant School 2000-2001
Site—Based Management Team Grant School—1996-98

Civic Plaques Received and Community Awards Involvement-Committed to bettering my community via volunteer work, civic activities, Events Coordinator, and Public Relations Secretary for 8 years with AIM/H (Association of Interested Minorities) **Citations from N J Legislatures-Ewing Township and the Mayor of Trenton for Outstanding Community Service Award—2010**

Citations from Senator Shirley Turner—Outstanding Community Leader
Citation from State of New Jersey Senate and General Assembly woman Watson Coleman
Grant Writing Certification—Sponsored by Research Associates, Columbia, S.C. Professor Edwin P. Davis **, M.Ed-Senior Certified Grant Specialist**
1992~ lst. Music Recital~ received plaque from Jenkins Brothers Music Development Center for producing first music recital.
1984—Fashion Designer Award—featured in Central Jersey Magazine as one of Trenton's designing women.
1983—Nominated Outstanding Young Woman of America-NAACP Award 1983
1983-Community Service Plaque-Black History Community Award-from E Trenton Civic Assoc.